To:

_____

From:

_____

Date:

_____

Espresso for the Soul

Published by Christian Art Publishers
PO Box 1599, Vereeniging, 1930, RSA

© 2013
First edition 2013

Designed by Christian Art Publishers

Images used under license from Shutterstock.com

Scripture quotations are taken from the *Holy Bible*, New Living Translation®, second edition. Copyright © 1996, 2004 by Tyndale House Publishers, Inc., Carol Stream, Illinois 60188. All rights reserved.

Scripture quotations are taken from the *Holy Bible*, New International Version® NIV®. Copyright © 1973, 1978, 1984, 2011 by International Bible Society. Used by permission of Zondervan Publishing House. All rights reserved.

Scripture quotations are taken from the New King James Version. Copyright © 1979, 1980, 1982 by Thomas Nelson, Inc. Used by permission. All rights reserved.

Printed in China

ISBN 978-1-4321-0679-9

© All rights reserved. No part of this book may be reproduced in any form without permission in writing from the publisher, except in the case of brief quotations in critical articles or reviews.

13 14 15 16 17 18 19 20 21 22 – 10 9 8 7 6 5 4 3 2 1

Count life
by smiles,
not by trials.

Those who bestow **kindness** are **happy** and know the true meaning of **life**.

Never put a **question mark where God has** put a period.

Do not resist change, it's a door to new opportunities.

Be made new
in the attitude
of your minds;

put on
the new self,

created
to be like God in
true
righteousness
and holiness.

Eph. 4:23-24

Tomorrow

can only be changed
if you start changing
whatever is not right
today.

Give someone **HOPE,** it may be the only thing that they **desperately need.**

After failure,

the hope in

helps you to make

a fresh start.

Kindness adds value to life. The more you *give,* the more you *receive.*

Never tire of doing what is good.

2 Thess. 3:13

Wishing for better days is lamentable sliding;

To start changing is supremely gliding.

To change the negative atmosphere of your world is possible by changing the atmosphere of your MIND.

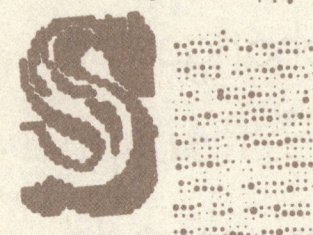

If anyone is in Christ, he is a new creation; the old has gone, the new has come! 2 Cor. 5:17

Change should not be seen as catastrophe; it is an opportunity for an exciting activity.

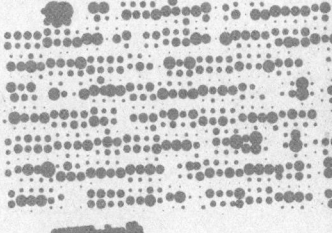

Change, like rock climbing, is hard and risky, but the view from the summit is enchanting

Set your minds on
things above,
not on
earthly things.

Col. 3:2

Kindness

is a happy
tune you have to
write the lyrics for.

To say to yourself,
"I will change for the better"

without

any action is like a
cloud blowing over the desert
without dropping any rain.

*The proof of the saying
is in the gaining.*

Do not try to change yourself from the outside in.

Instead, fill your mind with God's thoughts about you, which are

Fix your thoughts on what is **true**, and **honorable**, and **right**, and **pure**, and **lovely**, and **admirable**.

Think about things that are excellent and worthy of praise.

Phil. 4:8

Change your mindset and you change the way you perceive others.

Blaming your past
for who you are
will not change the
person you are into
the person you can become.

People who say,
"I'll have it my way"
display foolishness.
To pronounce,
"God has the final say"

that's wisdom.

True wisdom

is founded on knowing

and obeying God.

Teach us to number our days, that we may gain a heart of wisdom.

Ps. 90:12

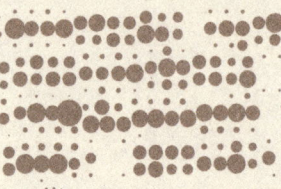

Growth in wisdom comes from a deepening relationship with God through personal experience.

If you look for a brighter morning, shaking off all gloom and mourning. Embrace wisdom, not earthly wealth, for a life of bounty and spiritual wealth.

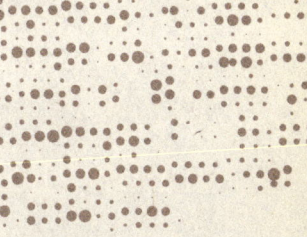

The LORD gives **wisdom;** from His mouth come **knowledge** and **understanding.**

Prov. 2:6

Wisdom

is like a fountain
of refreshing waters;
happy are those
who constantly
drink from it.

"Look before you leap"
is the *wisdom*
of some.
"Nothing ventured,
nothing gained"
is the wisdom of others.

Heed both.

Knowledge is knowing right from wrong.

Wisdom

is to make the right decision to keep you from doing wrong.

Wisdom

is a deep stream of

thoughts ...

... it refreshes all who immerse themselves therein.

If you need
wisdom,
ask our generous God,
and He will
give it to you.

James 1:5

T*G*I*F

Thank God I'm Forgiven.

How about you?

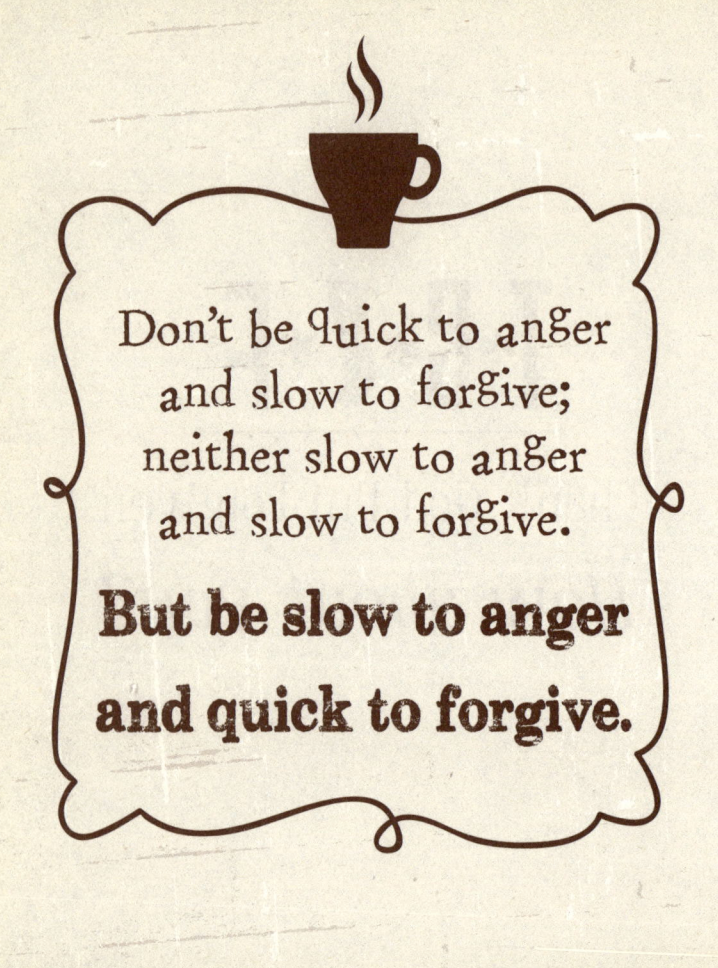

Don't be quick to anger
and slow to forgive;
neither slow to anger
and slow to forgive.

**But be slow to anger
and quick to forgive.**

Be kind and compassionate to one another, **forgiving each other.**

Eph. 4:32

The only way to empty the bitterness of the ♥ heart is by drinking from the ☕ cup of forgiveness.

To converse with grudge *a while*
Is many a time as humans *our trial.*
But the secret to enjoy life's *summit*
Is to forgive time and again *without limit.*

As far as the east is from the west, so far has He removed our transgressions from us.

Ps. 103:12

Time doesn't heal

the wounded heart –

the balm of

forgiveness

applied with prayer does.

Forgiveness -

the power stronger than that of revenge,

though harder to have power over.

"If you forgive other people
when they sin against you,
your heavenly Father
will also forgive you."
Matt. 6:14

Anybody can take revenge —
only the bold can forgive!

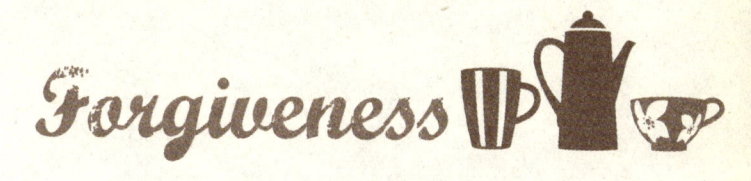

Forgiveness cannot change the unpleasant event, neither the past. It changes you and equips you for a *better future,* your grief to outlast.

"When you stand praying, if you hold anything against anyone, forgive them, so that your Father in heaven may forgive you your sins."

Mark 11:25

Thank God for what you have.
Trust God for what you need.

Hope is the gentle rain falling from heaven on a parched land, causing plants to grow and flowers to bloom.

Hope in a person's heart and the sun shining in its full glory has one thing in common – it brightens a dreary day.

Hope

No one who hopes in You will ever be put to shame. Ps. 25:3

Hope is not the answer to a problem

but a promised solution

that you believe in.

It is mercy, a gift from God

to hold on to as a drowning

person clutches at a straw

in a raging flood.

Be considerate and kind to others. It's a sound basis for building happiness — theirs and yours.

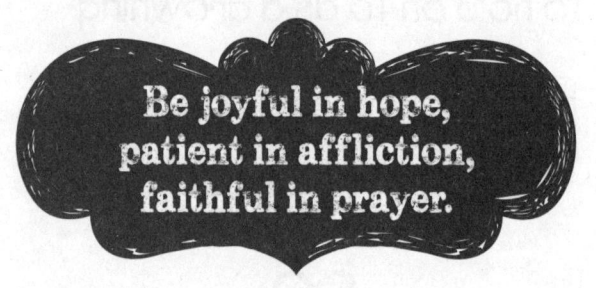

Be joyful in hope, patient in affliction, faithful in prayer.

Rom. 12:12

Hope is the *wings* that enable you to rise to the fulfillment of your *dreams* against all odds.

Kindness softens your face and makes light shine from your eyes.

I wait for the LORD, my soul waits, and in His Word I put my hope.

Ps. 130:5

Hope is not a big fire

beside which you sit to

warm yourself.

It is rather a small flame

shining in a dark night

to prove the existence of the

light of hope.

Faith in God germinates from the seed of hope that you Plant in sPite of the fruit that you do not see as yet.

May the God of hope fill you with all joy and peace.

Rom. 15:13

Hope is like the sun — dispelling the darkness of gloom.
The most powerful force on earth.

... is like firewood that you carry along with you. Wherever you go you can set the place aglow.

Love is God's gift to humanity;

the wine that fills

our cup of joy

to overflowing;

a foretaste of heaven;

a journey

without a station.

It's savored in the soul

but borne in the

heart.

God is love.

1 John 4:16

Love matters most

where it's needed most –

everywhere.

Never owe others anything but love and make sure the bill is never settled.

Love never fails.

1 Cor. 13:8

Since *love* is the very essence of God's character, it has no beginning and *no end.*

True love has no hidden agenda.

Greet

each other

with

Christian love.

1 Pet. 5:14

It's easy to stand with the crowd. It takes *courage* to stand alone.

Courage

is to keep on keeping on,
even in the face of evidence
contrary to gaining the

victory.

Courage is like a kite. The more of the wind's mounting, the more of the kite's surmounting.

The LORD is my strength and my song. Exod. 15:3

Be of good heart
in times of trouble.
If courage fails,
what hope is left?

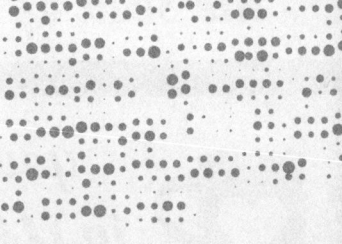

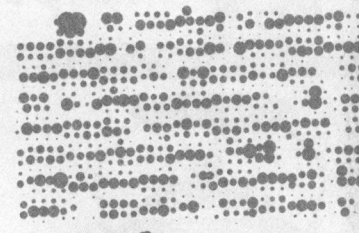

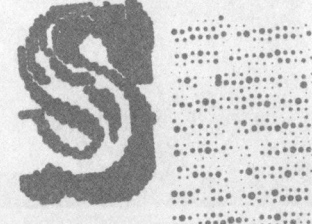

Courage germinates from the seed of faith in God that you plant in your heart.

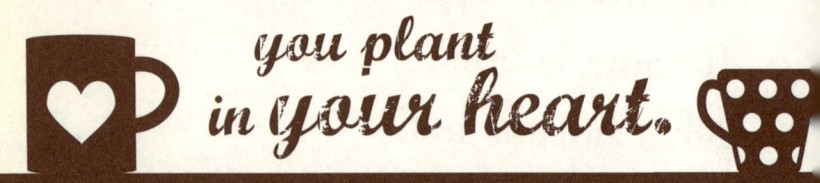

A skipper can't test his skills unless he has the courage to leave the safety of the harbor.

Faith in God
puts a sword of
courage
in your hand
to conquer the
giants in the land
of hopelessness.

A burning desire to make something more of your life according to the will of God, and the courage to rise after every demise, is the secret of a **winning attitude.**

There is life after failure.

Reposition your strategy in view

of what you've learned,

get rid of the lead in your feet,

reinforce your courage

with the steel of faith in God

to stand strong and

move forward!

When I called,
You answered me. Ps. 138:3

Courage

is to walk

in

boots of

faith.

Character

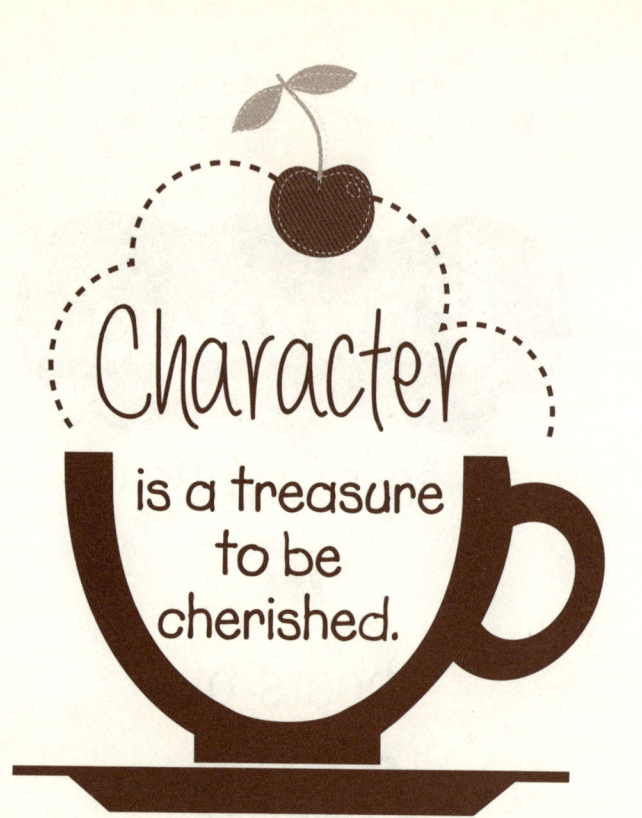

is a treasure to be cherished.

Endurance develops strength of character, and character strengthens our confident hope of salvation. Rom. 5:4

Character is reflected not in quantity of characteristics but in quality of heart

It takes time to build character.

It is lost in a *moment's* folly.

As any thought
is father to the deed,
so godly thoughts produce
good character,
whilst evil thoughts produce
bad character.

Do not be misled:
"Bad company corrupts
good character."

1 Cor. 15:33

If you've failed,

it doesn't mean

that you are a failure.

Not your achievements,

but your response to

setbacks, is the real proof of

character.

The constant dripping of water

wears away stone.

Likewise, seemingly insignificant

but wrong influences

can erode one's character.

Character is to behave amongst foreigners as if amongst friends.

The integrity of the upright guides them, but the unfaithful are destroyed by their duplicity.

Prov. 11:3

As a house built without a foundation won't withstand the tempest, so a man without character sinks in the storms of life.

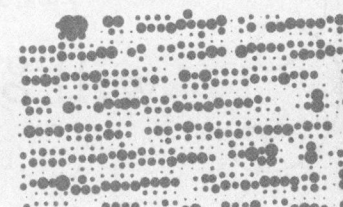

"By standing firm you will gain life."

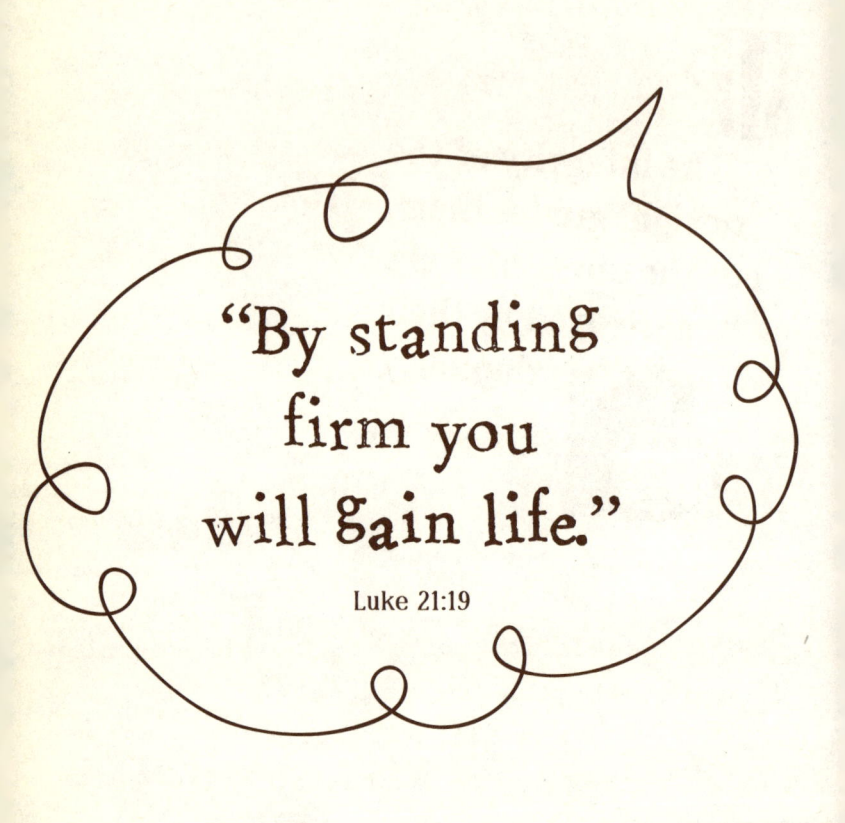

Luke 21:19

A wise person's character is known by the way they act.

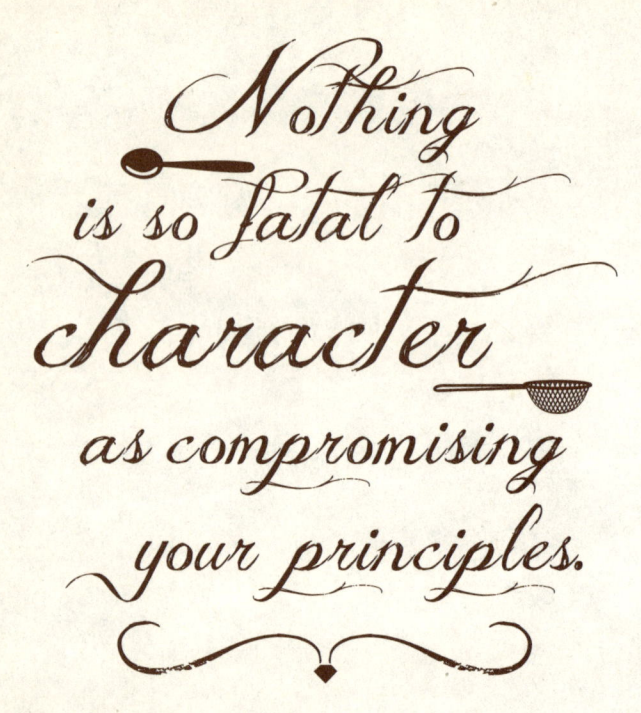

Nothing is so fatal to character as compromising your principles.

The godly walk with integrity;
blessed are their children
who follow them.

Prov. 20:7

A folly thought harbored in your mind can ruin character as a small leak can sink a ship.

> I know, my God, that You test the heart and are pleased with integrity.
>
> 1 Chron. 29:17

Character is betrayed by what a person finds to laugh at.

Rather have integrity unfold than riches untold.

A poor man of integrity is destined to bloom.

Pursue righteousness, faith, love and peace.

2 Tim. 2:22

Today is non-refundable ... make it unforgettable.

Integrity

is to sow seed of

truth even if you

are plowing

a lonely furrow.

Happy is the man
who keeps his word
even to his own hurt.
For he shall spend all

of

his days amidst

the noble of

heart

The fruit
of the Spirit is
love, joy, peace, forbearance,
kindness, goodness,
faithfulness, gentleness
and self-control.

Gal. 5:22-23

Stolen fruit is sweet, they say.

But the bitterness of regret

will long be remembered

after the thrill

of a moment's folly.

Character

is to avoid dishonesty, not because you can't get away with it, but because you know you won't be able to get away from yourself afterwards.

A person's greatest wealth lies in developing their character and potential.

Don't view shortcomings
as weak traits;
see them as attributes
with potential for development.

Never

again will I say,
"I cannot."
God has created a wealth
of potential in me

and

gave me the responsibility
to develop it to reign over the
vicissitudes of life.

It is *important* to know what you do, but it is *more important* to know and to do what you are able to do.

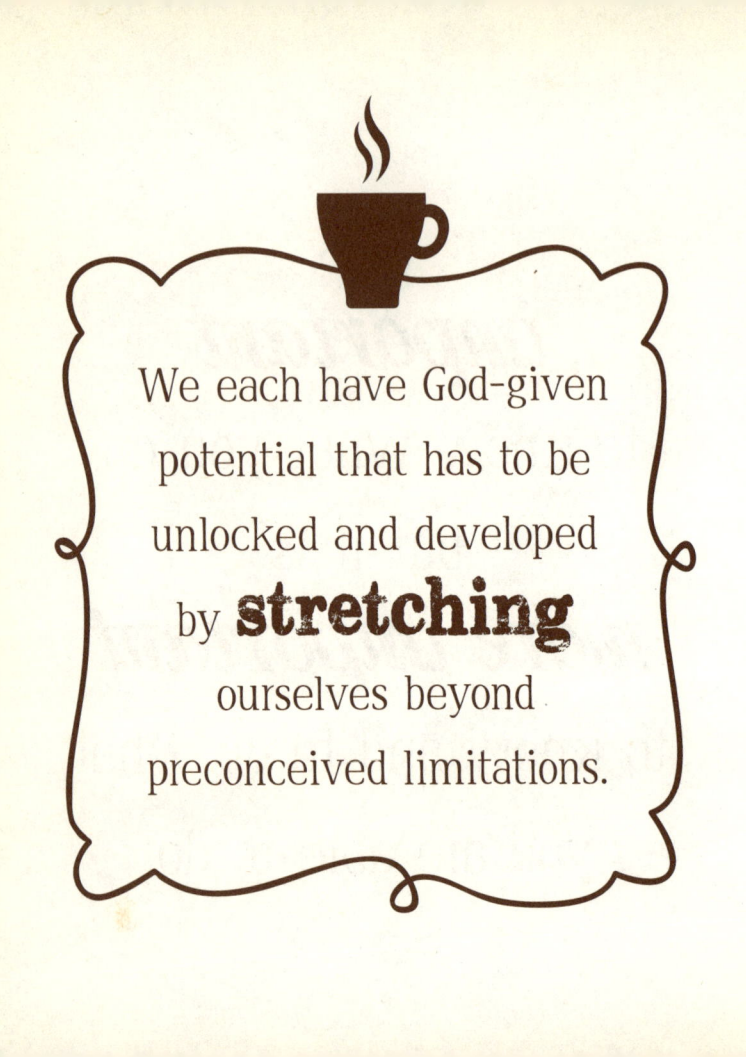

We each have God-given potential that has to be unlocked and developed by **stretching** ourselves beyond preconceived limitations.

Discover and develop your potential.
It is an adventure of discovery and enrichment in which you never fully arrive.

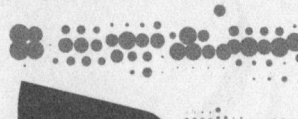

Be kind to others.

It's the

healing therapy

that they might need.

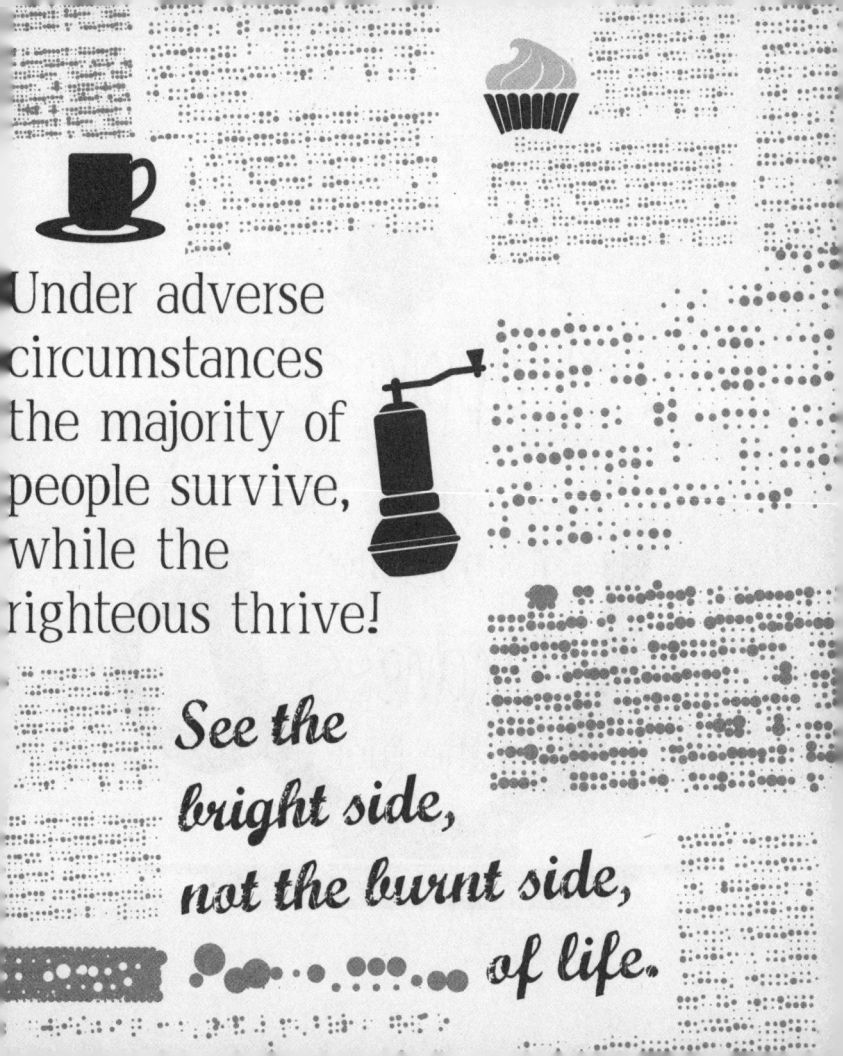

Under adverse circumstances the majority of people survive, while the righteous thrive!

See the bright side, not the burnt side, of life.

Happiness

is not a picnic spot —
it's a journey.

Kindness

is the fuel.